CHRISTOPHER DERRICK

Church Authority and Intellectual Freedom

CHRISTOPHER DERRICK

Church Authority
and
Intellectual Freedom

IGNATIUS PRESS   SAN FRANCISCO

With ecclesiastical approval
© Ignatius Press, San Francisco 1981
All rights reserved
ISBN 0-89870-011-6
Library of Congress Catalogue Number 81-80209
Printed in the United States of America

This book is an extended and otherwise modified version of four talks, given at Marquette University, Milwaukee, in March 1980.

I would like to express my gratitude for the hospitality and the intellectual stimulation which I enjoyed there, with particular mention of Fr. Richard R. Roach, S.J., Mr. Chauncey Stillman, and Mr. Harry John.

Wallington   *Christopher Derrick*
Surrey, England   *May 1980*

Chapter One

The title of this essay will probably remind my readers of a happening which received much publicity and aroused strong feelings in late 1979, and which may well have been followed by further and broadly similar happenings by the time this book appears in print.

The event which I have in mind looked—to many people—like a head-on collision between Church authority and intellectual freedom. Two well-known theologians were involved, each of them holding a senior academic post: Dr. Edward Schillebeeckx at Nijmegen, Dr. Hans Küng at Tübingen. Over the years, each of them had arrived at certain conclusions, concerning matters lying within a theologian's academic competence, and had published these in the normal fashion of scholars: thus and otherwise—notably at the Second Vatican Council—each of them had become very influential within the Roman Catholic Church and elsewhere too.

All scholars are accustomed to the experience of having their findings challenged, on intellectual grounds, by their academic peers. But the thing which happened to these two theologians, late in 1979, was of a different kind. They were challenged, and indeed called to order, by Church authority operating as such, and on lines which seemed to endanger the necessary intellectual freedom of all theologians and of Catholic thinkers and writers everywhere. With Pope John Paul II clearly behind it, the Congregation for the Doctrine of the Faith called the Catholic orthodoxy of Dr. Schillebeeckx very seriously in question and flatly denied the Catholic orthodoxy of Dr. Küng, with adverse consequences for the latter's position and career. Neither case has been fully resolved as I write these words, in April 1980, but the essentials of the situation are clear: Rome requires these two scholars to stop saying what they believe to be true, or at least to stop doing so in their capacity as Catholics and priests.

Such action, on Rome's part, was far from being unprecedented: it might be argued that by historical standards, these two theologians were treated with extraordinary gentleness and patience. But if we except the rather different case of Archbishop Lefèbvre, it had been a long time since Rome had acted on anything like these lines: many people were surprised to find it doing so once again, and reacted vehemently to this twofold case and the principles there at stake. There was in fact a first-class row: in any number of articles, broadcasts, interviews on television, letters to the press, and so forth, opinions were expressed forcibly.

They were also expressed diversely, and on interesting lines. By no means all of the Catholic votes were cast in favour of Rome's action, and by no means all of the non-Catholic and even anti-Catholic votes were cast against it. But while the pattern of response was complicated, three main viewpoints could be distinguished within it.

In the first place, there were some—not all of them religious people—who took such disciplinary action for granted, as being occasionally necessary for any organisation which hopes to remain in being. The captain of a ship has the right and duty to discipline mutineers and even mere troublemakers among his crew: no firm will long tolerate a salesman or agent who goes round denouncing the product and recommending the competition instead: an army officer who flouts the rule-book and gives aid and comfort to the enemy will soon find himself in trouble, and rightly. For Roman Catholics in this world, the pope is universally recognised as the boss, the top authority: why should it be considered outrageous if he acts as such, directly or through his staff?

In the second place, there were many who reached a rather similar conclusion on more religious, less organisational and military lines. While intellectual or academic freedom is an important value, they said, it is not an absolute value: when necessary, it must always be subordinated to the far more important value of orthodoxy, of fidelity to the mind of Christ as found in the mind and tradition of his Church. In appropriate though regrettable circumstances, it is therefore entirely right and proper that Church authority should intrude upon the intellectual or academic freedom of theologians and set limits to it: otherwise the faithful are going to be misled. (A number of Protestants spoke in this sense, sometimes in terms which suggested a certain envy of the Catholics. If only they also had an authority which could take such firm action when necessary!)

Then, in the third place, there was the large and vocal body of those who regarded this as an inherently undesirable *kind* of action, all too characteristic of the Catholic past, wisely abandoned in more recent years, and wholly deplorable in this new version, no matter how grossly erroneous the thought of Dr. Küng and Dr. Schillebeeckx might be. On this view of the matter, intellectual freedom comes first and is an absolute. Our primary concern must always be for truth rather than for mere orthodoxy or mere tradition, valuable though these things are in their limited way; and the search for truth can only be conducted fruitfully in an atmosphere of total liberty. Any intrusion upon this—as by censorship, or by some externally imposed requirement that certain conclusions must or must not be reached, or by the rebuke of dissidents—will render the whole enquiry sterile, as well as being a sin against natural justice; and in any case, given the mental climate of our tolerant age, no such intrusion can possibly achieve its desired purpose. If Church authority attempts to control thought or speech, it can only succeed in making itself look ridiculous.

Those who took this view of the matter sometimes compared Rome's treatment of those two theologians with Moscow's treatment of its dissidents. To them, it seemed particularly ironic that a pope who spoke up so bravely for human rights elsewhere should deny his own people the basic human right of free thought and speech. Let him put his own house in order before preaching to the world!

These three responses to that twofold case differ sharply enough. But they have one thing in common. According to all three, the two values mentioned in my title—"Church authority" and "intellectual freedom"—are necessarily in conflict, at least where the theologian is concerned. Where that conflict becomes acute, one may desire the one or the other to prevail. But the conflict itself remains: it is a kind of datum, an absolute, stemming directly from the mere meaning of those four words. In so far as a man favours anything that can properly be called "Church authority"—in doctrinal matters, in faith and morals—it follows in logic that he can only favour "intellectual freedom" in some radically qualified sense; and the converse is no less inescapably true. So, if Church authority gives anybody the kind of treatment—more or less—which it gave to Schillebeeckx and Küng in 1979, this must necessarily amount to an intrusion upon what may accurately be called the academic or intellectual freedom of the theologian or other religious thinker. It may be a justifiable and proper intrusion, it may be an outrageous intrusion. But for better or for worse, an intrusion upon that freedom is what it must always be.

In practice, it may be possible to arrive at a rough working compromise—a kind of armed truce—between those two conflicting values, each of which claims to be an absolute. But as between them, in this life, we cannot hope for actual *peace* unless this were to be attained by total surrender on the one side or the other; and few Catholics would desire such an outcome.

An assumption in this sense seemed to pervade the whole controversy that followed upon Rome's action in 1979. It is my purpose, in this essay, to call that assumption in question, as a matter of principle and in general terms. (I have nothing to say about the merits or deficiencies of Dr. Schillebeeckx and Dr. Küng as individuals and Catholics and scholars, or about the specific procedures of what used to be called the Holy Office and—before that—the Inquisition.)

In order to call that assumption in question, I shall need to re-examine the relevant concepts and also a number of widely-cherished presuppositions. What I want to suggest may well seem like a mere paradox at first. I therefore ask my readers to be patient. There can of course be accidental misunderstandings and injustices in any matter which involves human beings. But allowing for these, it seems to me that in principle, such actions of Church authority do not intrude upon any freedom which the Catholic theologian can possibly have or desire. On the contrary, they are something which he ought to welcome: in principle, they add up to further instances of what gave him academic respectability in the first place.

I want to lay much initial emphasis upon that concept of academic or intellectual respectability, even though I may thereby be speaking slightly out of character. I have distinguished three basic patterns of response to Rome's action of late 1979, and one of these was based upon the appeal to

Catholic orthodoxy and tradition, as to a supreme value. This is in fact my own position. But it is not the starting-point from which I wish to argue my present case. I propose to approach my subject from the other end, and to speak of it—initially—not in terms of Catholic principle but in terms of the values which are cherished by the academic and intellectual community as such.

The point is that I am a Catholic by grace but a sceptic by nature, and something of a Voltairean sceptic at that. When I hear anything confidently asserted, especially in matters of religion, it is my first instinct to say "But how can you possibly make that assertion with such assurance? How can you be so sure that you're right, when you thus dogmatise about the mysterious ultimates? Prove your case!"

I take this to be a legitimate approach to matters of religion, though I am not so foolish as to suppose that it is the only or even the most practically important approach to them. It means that I shall be talking about theology as an academic discipline, a field in which reality can perhaps be apprehended and put into words, in which propositions can be true or false and can—hopefully—be *known* to be true or false within their limits. Theology is a great deal more than that in fact: it is (or can be) a spiritual as well as an intellectual discipline, a divine wisdom, even a mode of holiness. It concerns the substance of faith; and faith is much more than an assertion of propositional truth—though (I would emphasise) much *more* than that, not less. As Martin Buber and Gabriel Marcel and others have reminded us, "faith that . . ." must always be complemented and even governed by "faith in . . .": the example of Jesus authorises us to be keenly dialectical upon occasion, but it was not through dialectic or debate that God saw fit to save his people. Against everything of that kind, we must always remember to set the bloodstained Cross and the flames of Pentecost, the whole of what caused Blaise Pascal to burst out dementedly with his *Memorial*. Where the things of God are concerned, we are not talking about something neatly manageable, like algebra.

I need to claim legitimacy for my own more propositional and initially sceptical approach, because I take it to be somewhat out of fashion nowadays. In our time, there is a strong preference for faith as experience, and as shared or community experience in particular, and a consequent soft-pedalling—almost to vanishing-point in some quarters—of faith as propositional belief, as doctrine, as information. Hence, anything remotely like the old Penny Catechism, or Pope Paul's *Credo of the People of God*, comes to seem wholly irrelevant to the formation of a Catholic Christian: for that purpose, the only important thing is the shared experience of the faith-community.

Much could be said about this recent and (I think) very questionable development. If it were my main subject, I would wish to point out (for example) that while there is no arrogance in disseminating information—in telling people the factually Good News—there can be a great deal of implied arrogance in any attempt of some group to impose the pattern of its own shared and favoured experience upon others. It's one thing to say "This is the message which we were told to pass on to you": no more pride is involved there than in the humble work of the letter-carrier or the man from Western Union. But we Christians will be on morally thin ice if we appear to be saying something more like "Be like us! Feel as we do!"

But for my present purposes, it is enough to point out that if we are to consider the specifically academic and intellectual kind of freedom as it affects the Catholic theologian—or, for that matter, any Catholic in his capacity as a thinking man—it will be the specifically academic and intellectual aspect of religion that must chiefly concern us. We shall mostly be considering those elements in the theologian's total life and work which he has in common with scholars and scientists in other fields, with all men who work for the apprehension and the verbal expression of truth on intellectually coherent lines. I am not saying that the remainder of his life as a Catholic Christian is of secondary importance, but only that it lies beyond my present subject.

With these considerations in mind, let us pay closer attention to that question of the theologian's academic respectability.

It it a painful question but a real one. From my sceptical starting-point, let me beg my readers to bear constantly in mind the immense *prima facie* plausibility of religious scepticism—of looking upon all theologians with kindly derision, as men who claim to search the unsearchable and know the unknowable. The logical positivist went too far when he said that theological utterances were devoid of meaning: in order to reach that conclusion, he needed to re-define "meaning" in absurdly narrow terms which made his own utterances meaningless as well. But the sceptic or agnostic is on much stronger ground when he says that while theological utterances can have their sufficiently clear meanings, they cannot be made by an academically respectable thinker because we have no way of knowing whether they are true or not, on this side of the grave at least. We are all entitled to cherish our personal hunches and opinions and guesses, and to put these forward as such. But the university deals—we hope —in more objective and verifiable things, as does the responsibly intellectual community at large. The campus is no place for hunches and opinions and guesses.

Can theology be anything more substantial? In transcendentally religious matters, is there any possible basis upon which we can say, with full intellectual responsibility, that something actually *is the case*? Is there any real possibility of religious *knowledge*, as scholars and scientists understand that noun? Is some statement of the transcendental kind more likely to be true because the man making it is very learned? The theologian's title implies that he claims to be a learned man who undertakes teaching and research in the field of religious knowledge: can we really concede this claim and so grant him full academic respectability and a lawful place on campus, alongside the scholar and the scientist, and with a full share in the rightful privileges of their vocation?

It would seem not, as St. Thomas might say.

This is indeed a painful question, but one of great importance to my subject. If the theologian claims the specifically academic or intellectual kind of freedom, he does so on the grounds that he is engaged in the specifically academic or intellectual sort of activity. But is he so engaged in fact? Many people doubt or deny this, saying that he deals only in guesses and opinions and dreams and myths and fantasies, of great psychological and anthropological interest but of no more objective validity; a man who puts these forward as "knowledge" (they say) cannot be regarded as a serious thinker and has no rightful place on campus at all, except perhaps in some minor and strictly non-academic role, comparable to that enjoyed by the Poet-in-Residence.

I do not myself share this view of the matter. But I do want to emphasise its extreme surface plausibility. We listen respectfully when a historian talks to us about history, because although not omniscient or infallible, he is a learned expert in that field: so with the physicist when he talks to us about physics. But it is far from obvious that on those same lines, a man can become a learned expert in transcendental matters of faith and morals, and so command our respectful attention when he talks to us about the things of God.

Let me re-state this initial scepticism in slightly different terms. Consider the word "theology".

Its form suggests a kinship to "biology" (the study of *bios* or life) and "geology" (the study of *ge* or the earth): theology, therefore, would seem to be the study of *Theos* or God. But we face an obvious difficulty here. If we ignore the murmurings of certain epistemologically doubtful philosophers, there is a general agreement that life and the world actually exist and can be fruitfully studied. There is in fact a wide area of consensus about each, shared by all reasonably well-informed people. You could write an elementary textbook about either of them, for the use of schoolchildren, and while your affectionate colleagues would doubtlessly say that you had written it very badly, with just the wrong kind of emphasis and method, they would not question your basic facts.

But nothing similar is true of theology. A great many people of high intellectual standing maintain that *Theos* or God is incapable of being studied because he doesn't exist: others maintain that while he may well exist, possibly or even probably, he is wholly incapable of being "known"— or even "known about"—while we remain in this life. Any kind of discourse about him will therefore amount to nothing more than the hunches and intuitions and opinions which I mentioned earlier, and these can provide no basis for an intellectual consensus or for any academic respectability at all. You will therefore be unable to write that elementary textbook for schoolchildren, on non-contentious lines, if your subject is theology. It will either be written from the standpoint of some particular faith or denomination, in which case it will seem highly controversial in the eyes of others; or else it will be a simply human and descriptive book, not about God but about what different peoples have thought and said and done with reference to their various concepts of divinity. It may well turn out to be a very good and non-contentious book in this latter sense, reliably informative and fair to all parties: many such books exist in fact. But no such book will be about "theology" in anything like the etymological sense of that word.

Must theology therefore be written off, as an intellectually sterile enquiry? It might seem so. The relevant questions have been canvassed intensely, by first-class minds and for centuries and millennia. If the human mind was capable of arriving at hard knowledge concerning even the barest basics of the matter, it would surely have done so by now: there would be at least a limited consensus. But there isn't.

It would be pleasant to ease the pain of this conclusion by finding certain things, of the substantively religious and even theological sort, that *can* be said with confidence on the basis of pure empiricism or experience and the rigorous but unaided intellect. I shall do my best.

Can we prove the existence of God? There are certain senses in which I believe that we can, and certain further senses in which we hardly need to do so: I am rather sceptical about the existence of atheists, properly so called. But the fact remains that the world contains many people who describe themselves as atheists, and they cannot all be dismissed as being insincere or intellectually incompetent; and I am afraid that I have never heard of a single atheist—whether genuine or so-called—who was convinced of his error and came to believe in God by any strictly rational process, as (for example) by finding himself unable to refute the cogency of St. Thomas's Five Ways. Atheists do cease to be atheists, but seldom or never like that. So, perhaps, with the immortality of the soul, our responsibility before God, and the alarming prospect of judgment. These beliefs can be rationally defended, even in the absence of any revelation, and various versions of them come more or less naturally to many peoples. But they can also be questioned or denied by thinkers of high integrity: they hardly add up, in practice, to fully demonstrable knowledge.

There are three senses in which religious knowledge is sometimes claimed, on some empirical or experiential basis rather than through revelation or as an end-product of pure reasoning. In the first place, it is said that the dead can speak to us from beyond the grave, through human and other intermediary agencies, thus assuring us of their survival and telling us something about our future destiny. In the second place, it is pointed out—perhaps with less assurance, nowadays, than when *The Golden Bough* made its first impact upon the world—that the myths and rituals of pre-scientific man speak in a remarkably consistent way about the ultimates of our condition and, in particular, about the Dying God or Mortal-Immortal who is our salvation, and who is some-how to be equated with the grain of wheat that dies in the soil and rises again in the spring to be our daily bread. Along with Jung's archetypes, do such things perhaps indicate that natural humanity has a direct (if confused) apprehension of transcendental reality, and even of something rather like Christianity? And thirdly, what are we to make of the remarkably unanimous testimony of the mystics, and of the possibly related testimony offered by those who practise "the expansion of consciousness" by less formally religious methods?

These three modes of experience are certainly interesting and suggestive: it would be foolish to dismiss them out of hand. But they hardly provide any sufficient basis for fully confident belief: they are too vulnerable to adverse criticism. Spiritualism is not totally invalidated by the fact that its history has included much fraud; but schizophrenia, and the very understandable if unconscious self-deception of the bereaved, are possibilities which cause its findings to be always questionable. In my view, it would also be unscientific to rule out the occasional relevance to it of diabolical possession; and I would add that so far as my own reading goes, these alleged messages from the Beyond show a marked tendency to reflect—very obviously—the mental "set" of those through whom they are said to be mediated, and also to be excruciatingly *dull*. If a theology were to be erected upon them, would its content go far beyond platitudinous uplift?

The common element in most mythologies and in most mystical and similar experiences is certainly striking. But if we start cold and with no previous commitment, can we be sure that this reflects anything more substantial than a tendency of the human mind to fool itself on very much the same lines, in suitable circumstances, no matter what its cultural background may be? Do such things tell us something about God, or only about the brain and its workings, even its pathological workings? "By prayer and fasting and other spiritual exercises, the pure in heart can come to see and even taste the One, the Lord of all things": I myself believe that statement. But I would find it very hard to prove a man wrong if he reduced it to some such form as "Self-hypnosis and chronic malnutrition, in conjunction with self-inflicted psychosomatic stress in other versions, generate patterns of hallucination which are always broadly similar."

On the most favourable interpretation, such experiences provide the theologian with some very intriguing possibilities; and an experimental or empirical quality can be cautiously attributed to them. But as far as I can see, nothing of that sort offers anything like the rigour and certainty which the scientist gets—ideally at least—from his repeatable experiment when made under controlled conditions; and if it did, the fact would offer the Christian theologian more embarrassment than vindication. All such approaches are ruled out by the terms of his faith: "Thou shalt not try experiments on the Lord thy God."

If a degree of religious consensus were to be established, none the less, on the three bases mentioned, it would be a very limited consensus: it would only be to the effect that some very odd things happen in our universe, inexplicable in terms of nineteenth-century scientific rationalism. The full-blooded materialist might then lose face to some degree: he is a rather unusual character anyway, a possibly endangered species. But if he sustains a loss, the theologian will not necessarily enjoy any corresponding profit. His academic respectability will remain as questionable as before: to the rigorously sceptical thinker, it will still be apparent that God (if he exists) cannot be known or studied in this life, at least as the university understands "study" and "knowledge".

From the sceptic's point of view, the matter can be stated very simply. Theology purports to be an academic field, an intellectual discipline: it is certainly a field in which hypotheses can be formulated very easily, and have been so formulated since the dawn of time, often in marked contradiction with one another. But on this side of the grave, the hypotheses so formulated, although they may be tremendously interesting and suggestive, cannot be tested at all. They can illuminate our imaginations and alter our lives by what *might be* the case: they give us no help at all towards knowing what actually *is* the case.

Hence, theology must always lack that academic respectability which other disciplines earn by being subject—at every point—to verification or falsification as the case may be.

In practice, theology shows a marked tendency to avoid this harsh judgment by subtly changing the nature of its subject-matter, and even by changing its name. In many universities, what was once called the "Department of Theology" is now called the "Department of Religion" or "of Religious Studies". The theologian adopts (in fact) the second of the two options that were open to you when you attempted to write a non-controversial school-book about his subject: his field now becomes an empirically descriptive and historical one, concerned not so much with God himself but with "religion" as a human preoccupation and activity. His primary concern will now be man—believing man, worshipping man, morally judgmental man, ecclesiastical man. This will provide him with an immense and useful field of study and also with unquestionable academic respectability, of the sort naturally and rightly accorded to those who work in the descriptive human sciences. He will be able to tell you (to take a very simple example) that while the Christians believe that there are three persons in one God, the Jews and Moslems most emphatically do not: he will be able to give you the history of all three belief-systems, to draw out their respective implications, to analyse their historical influence, all on very interesting lines. His learning has made him into an expert on beliefs about God.

But he will seldom claim, nowadays, that it has

made him into an expert on God. He will doubt-lessly have his personal faith, but this will be a strictly off-campus, non-academic affair. It was not as a believer in one faith or another that he secured his position: the university would not tolerate anything like the imposition of a reli-gious test upon applications for academic posts. So if you ask him whether the Christians or the Jews and Moslems are actually *right* about that fully transcendental and theological doctrine of the Trinity, he will not—in his academic capacity —be able to tell you.

He has secured his academic respectability, but at a price: there is no territory of the mind which he can call his own. "Religious Studies", after all, are only one specialised area within the territory of the descriptively human sciences in general: our theologian is obliged to share it with psychol-ogists and anthropologists and various others. So in the hope of greater autonomy, he may decide to concern himself also with the limited but cru-cial field of "natural religion", and notably with the existence of God. But even here he cannot reign alone: he will be told that all such questions are logically pre-religious and pre-theological in nature and therefore belong to the Department of Philosophy.

Within the officially agnostic university, he thus becomes something of an anomaly, a misfit, a displaced person: a landless man, possessing no such field as the word "theology" appears to suggest, tolerated—so long as he behaves himself and keeps a low profile—in fields that mostly belong to other people.

The human intellect has its limitations. No amount of learning and thought, unless helped from elsewhere, can give us a sufficient basis for saying responsibly that there are, or are not, three Persons in the one God.

The same goes for all other questions of that transcendental kind, including some which we may be disposed to regard as particularly urgent at our particular moment in history. We shall want these answered, and theologians and the Catholic intelligentsia in general will not be able to answer them. If they attempt to do so, they will be going beyond the limits of their competence and thus sinning against the academic code.

I shall mention three such questions, much canvassed recently and more controversial—even among Catholics—than the doctrine of the Trinity.

Can a woman become a priest?

It is clear that a bishop would encounter no physical difficulty if he saw fit to perform the rite of ordination upon a female subject, and that the lady in question would be able to go through the motions of saying Mass and hearing confessions afterwards. But would anything happen at either stage? If it comes to that, what "happens" when a man is ordained, and when he says Mass and hears confessions afterwards? In no such case can anything be empirically or experimentally shown to have happened: how far can unaided erudition of the theological kind cast light upon such questions?

It will certainly be able to tell us a great deal about the history of the belief that priesthood is an essentially masculine thing, closely involved with the concept of fatherhood and therefore with sexuality, so that a woman can no more become a priest than a man can become pregnant: the subject is an interesting one, and will take us not only deep into history but also into much of the territory definable as "Religious Studies"—into psychology, anthropology, comparative religion, and so forth. It will doubtlessly be suggested at some point—perhaps with emphasis—that this belief in an essentially male priesthood is a fruit of cultural conditioning, and only prevails in historic Christianity because Christianity grew up in male-dominated societies. But this, if true, will prove nothing: if it points in the one direction, it points in the other direction as well. It is often said nowadays that women can and should become priests: is not this also a culturally-conditioned phenomenon, stemming naturally enough from the preoccupation with equality and feminism which characterises our time? Perhaps so, perhaps not: either way, the substantive question still remains unanswered. About the psychological and social factors that predispose people to accept or reject some transcendental belief, erudition can tell us a great deal: about the actual truth or falsity of that belief, it can tell us nothing.

It is reasonable to ask whether a woman is capable of becoming a Catholic priest in the full sacramental and sacrificial sense of the term, because if she is, there's a great deal to be done. But the responsible thinker has only two options in this matter. He can resign himself to agnosticism; or he can have recourse to some fully transcendental source of information, if anything of that kind exists. Neither way will theological or other scholarship be able to give him any help at all.

Then, consider the much-canvassed but (to my mind) unsavoury question of contraception. About the medical, psychological, social, economic, demographic, and similar aspects of that question, suitably-qualified experts can talk freely and with authority, and do. But we can also pose the question in fully religious or transcendental terms, and ask "Is contraception always—or sometimes, or (in itself) never—contrary to God's will for us?"; and if we do, there is no possible basis upon which any kind of scholar or scientist can reply with the authority of his *expertise*. Any answer to *that* question—and it's the question which the Christian conscience will primarily need to have answered—will need to be based upon some totally different kind of authority. (I would add, in passing, that this should have no absolute need to be papal. Where the erotic sensibility of society at large is in a reasonably healthy state, the common Christian conscience will be able to answer the question for itself. But the erotic sensibility of society at large is not always in a reasonably healthy state.)

Finally, let me mention the numerous and varied developments which have taken place in the Catholic Church since the Second Vatican Council. These are fully capable of being studied descriptively, and also of being evaluated by any preferred human criterion. But what if people assert —as some people often do—that certain of these developments, favoured by themselves, are also favoured by the Holy Spirit and are in fact manifestations of the Holy Spirit in action, whereas contrary developments are not? I have heard such claims made for the development represented by Dr. Küng: I have also heard them made for the development represented by Archbishop Lefèbvre. One may well have personal sympathies in this direction or that; but one's personal preferences are only psychological facts about oneself and prove nothing. Is there any more objective basis upon which, in this matter, a serious thinker can distinguish the operations of the Holy Spirit from the operations of more questionable factors —of human restlessness and intellectual pride, of a desire to be with the trend? If there is, it clearly cannot be academic in nature, a matter of intelligence and learning. The Holy Spirit blows where he chooses and fills the whole world: his operations are hardly to be captured in texts, tracked by radioactive isotopes, analysed by computer.

About those three currently-disputed questions, as about the Trinity and the whole range of transcendental belief, certainty must come from some transcendental source or not at all.

I do not want the sceptic to have the last word, but I do want him to have this first word. My subject is intellectual freedom, as this concerns theologians and the Catholic intelligentsia at large.

I do not wish to suggest that the government, or any comparable agency, should control or oppress those who deal frankly in mere opinions, dreams, and fantasies. But when we attach high importance (as I do) to the specifically academic and intellectual kind of freedom, we are normally claiming it on behalf of people who are engaged in enquiries of some more substantial kind, in one version or another of the search for truth or certainty, and *because* they are so engaged. This is something over and above the ordinary freedoms which we desire all men to enjoy: its ultimate basis is the sacredness of truth.

When we invoke this sacred principle in the theologian's favour, we must therefore remember that the sceptic is partially right. It is not wholly obvious that theology, properly so called, is an intellectually respectable discipline and can claim to be treated as such. Learning of any kind is of course a good thing: when of the theological kind, it can be among the things that help us to understand any possible assertion of faith in progressively greater depth—though in this respect, prayer and suffering will often be quite as useful. But no kind of learning (strictly as such) can contribute to theological *knowledge* in any full sense of that word, on lines that would provide us with a sufficient basis for the actual affirmation or denial of any possible transcendental belief, any article of faith. When it comes to such an affirmation or denial, the greatest theologian in the world is—so to speak—reduced to the ranks. Whether his faith-assertions are of the most rigidly "conservative" or the most far-out "liberal" sort, he then speaks with no special authority: his learning makes him no more likely to be right than the rest of us.

I do not believe that the sceptic is entirely right, however; and I shall now turn to the basis upon which the Catholic theologian can be accorded full academic respectability, after all, and to the consequences which follow for his academic or intellectual freedom.

But let us not forget the initial plausibility of the sceptic's case. If we are invited to accept some belief of the fully transcendental kind on the ground that those proposing it are very intelligent and learned men, there are excellent *prima facie* reasons for responding with a broad objectionable sardonic grin. When human cleverness attempts to transcend its own limitations, it presents an amusing spectacle.

Chapter Two

If the theologian is to achieve academic respect-ability, he will need to have subject-matter of the kind suggested by his title and also an appropriate methodology for handling it, a verification-method in particular. He will therefore need to start from a faith-position of some kind; and if he is to be called a Catholic theologian, this will need to include the concept of Church authority. Each of these requirements is capable of being misunderstood and demands careful consideration.

Certain sensitivities of our time mean that almost any use of that word "authority" is likely to evoke an immediate and sharply negative response, as though some kind of tyranny were being proposed. It is therefore important to remember that the word has two distinct senses: here, I am only concerned with one of them.

Every human institution, from a family to an empire, involves at least some measure of "authority" in the disciplinary sense. There has to be law and order, there must be at least some rules and at least some occasional enforcement of them. "Authority", in this sense, is notoriously open to abuse. Power tends to corrupt: those who hold authority are constantly tempted to extend their power and use it tyrannically, which is why we find ourselves stuck with the insoluble problem of politics. But unfortunately, anarchism is not a real option. Individual freedom is immeasurably precious, but will prove self-destructive if made into an absolute.

Rightly or wrongly, justly or unjustly, "authority"—in this sense of the word—calls for a response of obedience. But there is a wholly distinct sense in which "authority" calls for a response of assent, of intellectual acceptance, even of faith. When we say that a learned man is a world-famous authority in his field, we do not mean that he gives commands and expects to be obeyed in respect of it: we mean that he knows what he's talking about, not totally or infallibly but to an exceptional degree. In the same way, if a college student makes some questionable assertion, his tutor may well reply "H'm—what's your authority for that statement?", with no implication that it was made in obedience to orders. We need "authority" in the former sense because of our tendency to behave badly: we need "authorities" in this latter sense because of our ignorance and our consequent need to consult and trust those who know more than we do.

The former and quasi-political kind of authority exists, visibly and historically, within the Catholic Church: it would be rash to claim that it has always been exercised with perfect justice and discretion—though in this respect, the Church's record is immensely less disgusting than the State's. But if I speak now of "Church authority" I have the second or doctrinal sense of the word in mind. Our starting-point was sceptical: if we want to study God and the things of God, as the word "theology" implies, we shall find ourselves frustrated by near-total ignorance unless we can find some "authority", some source of reliable information.

If we fail to find one, the sceptic will need to have the last word as well as the first, with unfortunate consequences for the theologian.

All mankind experiences a hunger for transcendental certainty, for unquestionably valid faith, far beyond what can possibly be provided by science or scholarship or philosophy and verified in any immediate way. In many, this hunger is so intense that they invent satisfactions for it, no matter how implausible these may seem to others.

These satisfactions have commonly been religious in the past: in our time, they are quite as likely to be political or ideological—though the last few years have seen a remarkable recrudescence of the most bizarre cultic and mystical certainties, not only in southern California.

This hunger can be seen in two ways. In the first place, it can be seen as a kind of mental perversion or sickness. On this reckoning, the wise man ought to accept the fact that dogmatic certainty of that transcendental kind is simply not available in this life: any desire to possess it will usually be a mere psychological weakness in ourselves, a childish desire to cuddle some security-blanket, or perhaps a thinly-disguised desire to dominate other people with one's splendid assurance. The trouble is that one cannot easily see how humanity has come to have such a strong desire for a totally non-existent object. We experience sexual desire, but there is sexual satisfaction: we experience hunger, but there is food. If there is no transcendental certainty, why should we want it? The problem becomes more acute if we see mankind in strictly evolutionary terms. Rough empiricism is what helps us to survive and so reproduce and pass on our genetic characteristics: transcendental certainty does not, nor does the desire for it. Faith can even make people into celibates and martyrs, and so militate—in a small way—against its own survival.

Alternatively, we can accept this desire or hunger as a legitimate fact about ourselves and then look around for its proper object. Thwarted desires often seek improper objects: the man who lacks a girl will sometimes make do with a boy, the hungry child will sometimes eat dirt. In each case, a proper object for the desire exists and can be specified without much difficulty. How can we specify the proper object of our desire for transcendental certainty? A great deal of dogmatism is easily recognisable as mere conceit and self-assertiveness: is there any possible certainty which we can properly make our own, without necessarily being guilty of those two faults?

This is not a book of Catholic apologetics, and I do not propose to offer here any justification of my own belief that Jesus, as found and lived in the faith of his universal Church, is for us—among many other things—the one-and-only proper object of the desire which I have been talking about: other satisfactions of that desire being incomplete or delusory in the measure of their distance or difference from Catholic Christianity, whatever subjective feelings of certainty they may provide. Nor do I propose to offer any long exploration of the relationship between faith and reason. But in that connection and for my present purposes, I need to mention two extreme positions which I reject.

The first of these is the idea that faith is something wholly irrational and arbitrary, a pure leap in the dark, and thereafter, a kind of sacred absolute about the person concerned. On this view, reasoned argument cannot support a man's faith and should never be used to criticise or attack it: to argue in favour of some "one true faith" is as grossly imperialistic as it would be to impose one's own tastes in food or poetry upon everybody else. Every faith is wholly valid for the man who commits himself to it, and he does this by arbitrary choice, an act of the pure will: it doesn't matter—in any objective sense—which faith he chooses, and plenty of them are available in the marketplace.

This view of things appeals strongly to those who understand "toleration" and "ecumenism" in the very un-Christlike sense of implying that in matters of religion, nobody can ever be found and declared mistaken. The trouble is that if religion is a field in which nobody can ever be wrong, it must also be a field in which nobody can ever be right. The sceptic will then have won the argument, after all, depriving the theologian of his subject-matter and thus of his intellectual respectability.

Against this view of the matter, I take the traditional Catholic view that while faith is indeed a choice, an act of the will, it is not simply that. In principle—and, according to the abilities and circumstances of the individual, in practice too—it needs to be directed by the intellect in the first place and also to be intellectually defensible thereafter.

But while I thus reject the view that faith is (or should be) wholly irrational, I also reject any suggestion that it can be wholly rational—that its content can be ascertained as the content of physics or history is ascertained, by purely intellectual methods operating upon empirical data. This was the theme of my first chapter: the content of faith is something *needed* by the relevant kind of intellectual expert, normally the theologian: it cannot possibly be something *provided* by him for our enlightenment. Faith itself is a gift from God, not the end-product of some long and perhaps syllogistic chain of argument: at the end of any such chain, the leap of faith still needs to be made. Reasoned argument of the apologetic sort cannot eliminate the necessity of that leap: it cannot coerce people directly into Catholicism.

There are two things which it can do. In the first place, it can show that the act of making that leap of faith is an essentially and indeed uniquely reasonable thing to do: it can cause this to be no longer a leap in the dark, a matter of *blind* faith, but a leap made in a certain measure of light, and into a much greater light. Secondly, it can show that the act of asking God for the gift of faith is not intellectually improper. The sceptic may be disposed to call it an offence against the integrity of the mind, an exercise in self-hypnosis and self-deception: it is one primary task of apologetics to refute this charge.

With these considerations in mind, I turn to the question of what we mean by "Catholic theology", and of what subject-matter will give academic respectability to its practitioners.

If both the noun and the adjective are to be given their full meanings, "Catholic theology" will need to be defined as that academic discipline which has for its subject-matter "God, in himself and in his operations and with various consequences for ourselves, as made known to us by the authority of Christ-in-his-Church"—the word "authority" having here its second sense, doctrinal and even informational. The primary datum or starting-point of Catholic theology is the premise that God is so made known to us, and reliably.

The terms of that definition can be varied within limits. The object of theological study can, for example, be defined in liturgically familiar words as "the Catholic Faith that comes to us from the Apostles"—from the original twelve in the first instance, and now from their successors the Catholic bishops, identified as such by their unity with the See of Peter: this faith, and the duty of bearing witness to it, being also diffused throughout the whole body of those who are faithful to it.

But in any version that will do full justice to the two words chiefly involved, our definition will have three consequences for the Catholic theologian. In the first place, Catholic faith has to be the starting-point of his enquiry, not one of its possible findings: its content is for him what experimental findings are for the physicist or original source-documents for the historian. In the second place, he has—in his academic capacity—no competence to deny (or, strictly speaking, to assert) anything put forward by the Church as a matter of faith. And finally, if he or anyone else decides that the Catholic faith is untrue or at least erratically and unreliably true—that God is *not* reliably and consistently made known to us by Christ-in-his-Church—he must not therefore conclude that the Catholic theologian ought to think, write, behave, and be treated in some different way. His proper conclusion, from that point of decision onwards, should be that Catholic theology is an unreal subject, which is what the sceptic or agnostic was telling us all along.

The sceptic or agnostic may well have an objection to raise at this point. Can academic respectability really be conceded to any discipline which depends, from start to finish, upon commitment to something as controversial as the Catholic Faith? Every kind of science and scholarship has for its subject-matter, its raw material, something which is accessible to all men if they care to look: in the enquirer, it demands no kind of previous commitment but only objectivity and intelligence and an open mind above all. Any closing of the mind, as by any kind of faith-commitment, must necessarily make the whole enquiry irrational and therefore (by academic standards) disreputable.

The trouble about this argument is that it proves too much: it undermines the respectability of nearly all disciplines, not only of Catholic theology. They also depend upon prior assumptions which are pre-rational or pre-scientific in nature, are incapable of being rigorously proved, and have in fact been questioned or denied by any number of perfectly sane people.

Take the natural sciences, for example. They depend upon observed phenomena: that is to say, they by-pass the whole question of epistemology and presume that the external world is actually *there*, more or less as we perceive it and independently of our perceiving minds. This presumption will cause the physicist some trouble when he gets down inside the atom, but he needs to retain it at the macroscopic level if he is to do any experimental work at all. Common experience is certainly compatible with this presumption or belief, which I happen to share. But common experience is also compatible with a good many other beliefs; and the philosopher will have some disquieting things to say about what the practical scientist happily takes for granted, as does the scholar or enquirer in any other field. Epistemological doubts, if they are to be entertained at all, will be as destructively valid in the library as they are in the laboratory. In practice, we by-pass them by an act of faith.

All scholars and scientists make a further act of faith in the general honesty of their colleagues and predecessors. You cannot repeat all the experiments, you cannot check all the source-documents for yourself: life is too short. And it is sad but true to say that even the world of science and scholarship includes recorded instances of hoax, of distortion, of deception, of downright lying. But we proceed in the faith that such things will be very exceptional, which they are certainly not in—say—politics. We also assume, without proof, that most peoples have been wrong in believing the visible universe to be full of spirits both friendly and hostile, whose influence upon phenomena will be real but imperceptible and immeasurable, so rendering all observations doubtful: we assume, further, that the laws of nature and of thought are equally valid throughout space and time. I do not wish to call any of these assumptions seriously in question, with the partial exception of those good and evil spirits. But let us remember that they *are* assumptions, acts of faith: they are not proved findings.

It may be replied that they work in practice, yield hard and consistent results where the contrary assumptions do not, and are thus validated empirically or by experience. But the philosopher will have some further disquieting things to say about the insufficiency of pragmatism as a guide to truth; and the Catholic theologian will be able to point out the extreme difficulty of showing that his Faith does not also "work".

The fact is that every possible enquiry—with

the possible exceptions of philosophy and pure mathematics—needs to begin at some point which will be questionable in logic, since nothing can be verbally asserted which is not also capable of being verbally questioned. Even philosophy faces this necessity in its way. It would doubtlessly be foolish, in practice, to ask Descartes how he *knows* himself to be thinking. But if we did, his only possible answer would be a logically unsupported yet perfectly sensible assertion.

The sceptic thus goes too far if he denies respectability to any discipline which depends upon some initial faith-position. But he may perhaps be allowed to make certain stipulations where any possible theology is concerned, and its theologians' desire to be accepted as serious thinkers. He will not be acting unjustly, for example, if he requires that the faith-position in question should have stood the test of time and achieved a certain position in the world of thought: he cannot be asked to concede respectability to every freak-out minority-cult of the moment. Nor can he be asked to take seriously a thinker whose faith-position is vague or inconsistent or demonstrably false, or is regarded as being too elusive and rarefied and fragile for rational discussion. If the theologian wants to live in the kitchen, he must be prepared to stand up to the heat: he must be willing to talk about his faith-position, to be explicit about its basis and content and methodology, to defend it against critical attack. It need not and indeed cannot be provable in any logically coercive sense, but it does need to be self-consistent and also compatible with whatever assured certainties are attained in other fields (though not necessarily with currently popular hypotheses and habits of the mind): it must stand up to being handled rather roughly in broad daylight.

These are exacting requirements, and they exclude various faith-positions that are widely held. But so long as the Catholic theologian proceeds consistently as such, and in full respect for the objective and determinate nature of his subject-matter, he gets by nicely. While still disagreeing with him, the sceptic can then be asked to concede him full respectability as a serious thinker, with all the scholarly privileges and freedoms which that respectability confers.

Any intellectual enquiry can be described as a respectful interrogation of one's subject-matter and a formulation and testing of hypotheses.

What the Catholic theologian interrogates may be called, briefly, "the mind of the Church", in which—on Catholic premises—the mind of Christ himself is to be recognised, the mind of

God: this is his primary "authority", in the sense of being his primary source of knowledge in matters otherwise unknowable.

But where is "the mind of the Church" located? How, in the concrete, does the theologian find his subject-matter? How can any of us distinguish the mind of Christ in his Church from the various patterns of merely human opinion that prevail from time to time among Catholics? As the communication-theorist might say, how do we distinguish "signal" from "noise", God's signal from man's noise? The Church is certainly a very noisy place, and perhaps more so nowadays than at some times in its often tumultuous past. It might help if we all talked a bit less, though I am quite the wrong person to say so: God may perhaps be finding it rather difficult to get himself heard. His voice is certainly not to be equated with those human voices which happen to be shouting most loudly at some particular moment.

At certain times in the past, it would have been necessary to point out here that the mind of the Church is not located simply and solely at Rome and embodied infallibly in every Vatican utterance. Some Catholics may still need a reminder in this sense. But there are others who need a reminder in more or less the opposite sense.

In this matter, our primary sources are classically named as Scripture and Tradition, with a delicate question arising as to whether these are to be regarded as a single *fons revelationis* or as two separate *fontes*. I would wish to make two points. The first is that the Church is both logically and historically anterior to the New Testament, which can accurately be called an early and partially definitive publication of the Church and expression of its mind. The second is that what we call Tradition—in a sense of that word which is rather technical and can be misunderstood—amounts to the collective mind and memory of a Church which is still alive and can still speak, so that we are not wholly dependent (for faith and morals) upon old books, as interpreted for us by the best modern scholars.

We have recently started to call this living voice the *magisterium*, a word which corresponds fairly closely to my second sense of "authority" but is confused by some with my first and disciplinary sense of it. The concept carries a more complex meaning than the ultramontane mind likes to suppose. The Pope can certainly speak with the mind and voice of the Church, infallibly upon occasion, and always so weightily as to demand a "religious submission of will and of mind".[1] But that

[1] Vatican II, *Lumen Gentium*, 25.

magisterium or authority is also to be found in the Fathers, and in theologians both living and dead, and in the ordinary teaching work of the bishops, more especially when they meet in council; and there is a further and crucial sense in which not only the Faith but the actual teaching authority of the Church is diffused throughout the whole body of the faithful, the People of God.

All this needs to be said, and was said by the Second Vatican Council. But unless care is taken, it involves a seldom-noticed danger of logical circularity, such as would cause "the mind of the Church" to elude all possibility of being ascertained and studied and the theologian to lose his subject-matter.

One instance of this circularity was implicit in the old Vincentian Canon. The mind of the Church is indeed diffused through the whole body of the faithful, as extended in space and time: the Faith is thus definable as "What is always, everywhere, and by all people believed". But who are the "all people" in question? They can only be "the faithful"—that is, those who are in fact true to the mind of the Church. This gets us nowhere, nor can any other appeal to the *consensus fidelium* if taken in isolation: such words must always beg the question.

So with the Fathers and Doctors of the Church. How do we tell the great Doctor from the great heresiarch? Certainly not by asking the man in question or the large body of his devoted followers: no man believes himself to be, or to be following, a heretic. If it comes to that, no man who wasn't mad with pride would ever set himself up as a Father or Doctor of the Church, instructing it on his own account. Such honourable titles are conferred later, by the Church and upon those whom it sees as having articulated its mind exceptionally well, if not always with perfect accuracy. (St. Thomas was wrong about the Immaculate Conception, and one can find startling things here and there in the Apostolic Fathers.)

The fact is that the ultramontane mind exaggerated something which is logically as well as theologically necessary if "the mind of the Church" is to have any ascertainable existence. In the Catholic tradition, that mind finds its ordinary expression in the ordinary *magisterium* of the Catholic bishops. But this tells us nothing unless we know who the Catholic bishops are; and unless we are to get trapped in further circularities, we shall need to identify them by their unity—doctrinal as well as canonical—with the Holy See.

I am not here concerned to offer any rehabilitation and re-assertion of the papal and Petrine office as a matter of doctrine. My point is a purely logical one. Without some such fixed and—if you like—arbitrary point of reference, the mind of the Church must always be something so fluid and undefinable as to rule out any effective knowledge and study of it.

This fact has bedevilled Anglican theology from the start, or at least since the Oxford Movement: I have recently written about the extent to which C. S. Lewis was a victim of it.[2] Where the papacy is played down, it also bedevils Catholic theology, rendering it intellectually incoherent and thus—by the sceptic's standards as proposed earlier —disreputable.

The average theologian of today is unlikely to make the ultramontane mistake of actually *equating* the Church with the papacy and (in practice) with "the Vatican". That mistake, if followed, would certainly make his task much easier, though much less interesting too: he would only need to write his hypothesis out on a slip of paper, insert this into the Roman computer, and see if it came out with a "yes" or a "no" stamped upon it. Ecclesiastical practice has sometimes taken a pattern which can be caricatured, not too unfairly, on those lines: we have there a distinctly

[2] Christopher Derrick, *C. S. Lewis and the Church of Rome: A Study in Proto-Ecumenism* (San Francisco: Ignatius Press, 1981).

insufficient "model" of the relationship between the theologian and the Church.

It is a useful model, even so, if only because it reminds us of what that relationship must necessarily be. As I have said, the Church's *magisterium* or teaching authority is partly to be found in the Fathers and Doctors and in theologians both living and dead. But the *magisterium* of such people must always be of a secondary kind. As scholars and thinkers—even of the first class—they can tell us nothing about transcendental matters: we do not believe what they say because they say it, but because the Church accepts and endorses it, and only in the measure in which the Church *does* accept and endorse it. This is notably true of Moral Theology, a field in which formal *de fide* pronouncements are not very numerous: if a legal analogy may be permitted, it resembles a vast mass of case-law, with little in the way of codification or statute. Hence, in this field, it is customary to speak of the "received" or "accepted" authors: these are the moral theologians whose thought has long been tested and accepted by the mind of the Church, as this confronts itself in a million confessionals.

My point is that in faith and morals alike, the theologian's task must always be a task of interrogation: the limitations of the unaided and unguided human intellect mean that it can never be a task of instruction or correction.

So I would like to offer another model of the relationship between the theologian and the Church, one that will do better justice to the interrogatory nature of his work. Let me compare it to the courtroom relationship between a cross-examining lawyer and a sworn witness. This is not a perfect analogy, since while a theologian will normally be part of the Church, a lawyer will seldom be part of the witness.

But we can see things fruitfully in those terms. The lawyer needs to be an intelligent and highly-trained expert: the witness needs only to have been there, to have seen it all, and of course to be honest and have a good memory. His testimony may originally have been blurted out in some very simple form: under skilled questioning it will not exactly change, but its full content and implications will be progressively drawn out so as to provide a far more detailed and explicit picture than was available at first, though not otherwise a different picture.

During this long process of what we may call "development", the lawyer will normally operate by putting to the witness a series of formulae, each one being a hypothetical interpretation of the matter in hand under one aspect or another; and to each of these the witness will respond—

sometimes by simple acceptance and agreement, sometimes by firm and perhaps angry denial, and often by further thought and the drawing of previously unnoticed distinctions.

The Church's testimony began with a single shout of "He is risen!"; and in nearly two thousand years, it has developed so richly that even a simple outline of Catholic doctrine—such as the *Credo of the People of God*, issued by Paul VI in 1968—must be a fairly lengthy document. And to a very considerable extent though not completely, this process has been a matter of the Church responding to cross-examination by learned theologians, sometimes in terms which declared them heretical.

One crucial part of it might be dramatised in the following way.

Lawyer: "I see—you're telling the Court that Jesus was a man like ourselves, specially favoured by God but quite distinct from him, the highest of created beings but no more than that?"

Witness: "No, no, you've misunderstood me. Jesus was and is the Lord—not a created being, not distinct from God!"

Lawyer: "I'm sorry, I didn't mean to misrepresent you. So what you've been trying to tell us is that Jesus was an apparition of God, looking like a man but not actually human—a sort of holy phantom? I'm sure the Court will appreciate the

deeper spirituality of this interpretation. Our
bodily nature, with all its obscene functionings, is
far too low and vile to be associated with the
Godhead, is it not?"

Witness (insistently and even angrily): "No! Once
again, you're putting words into my mouth!
Jesus is true God *and* true man: he has always
been the Son of God and—how shall I put it?—
'consubstantial' with the Father: that's the best
word I can think of at the moment. And just a
few years ago, without ceasing to be God, he was
born into this world as an actual man, bodily
functionings and all. And he doesn't share your
view of those functionings: when he set out to
liberate the world, he didn't shrink back from the
female generative tract, as though it were something disgusting!"[3]

So christology developed: so did the Church
reject both the Arian and the Docetist or Mono-
physite over-simplifications of its testimony, de-
claring these to be heresies. It made for a longer
Creed, but not otherwise for a different Creed:
the process has continued since then, and will
presumably continue until the world's end and
the Church's, the time of Judgment.

This model is indeed imperfect, in that the theologian is not wholly distinct from the Church.

---

[3] This is my own translation of a verse from the *Te Deum*.

But when on duty as such, he does—in a sense— go through the motions of distancing himself artificially from the mind of the Church and considering it critically and from the outside: he ceases (by convention) to be a believer and becomes simply a questioner. Hence St. Thomas— a believer if ever there was one—could put a question-mark after every possible doctrine.

The same principle was implied by the old and well-mannered convention by which a theologian submitted all his writings to the judgment of the Church—often explicitly, in a little printed note at the beginning of his book. It was as though he were saying "It's your mind that I'm trying to state and interpret, not my own—please tell me if I'm in any danger of misrepresenting you!"

Something of that kind is always good manners, when one sets out to speak on someone else's behalf. But for the theologian, it is also a logical necessity. In transcendental matters of faith and morals, his erudition gives him no possible basis for speaking out definitively on his own account. He is extremely skilled at asking good questions about such matters. But when it comes to the answering of them, he speaks with no more personal authority than a well-instructed Catholic child or peasant.

The lawyer can sometimes be justified in pressing the witness very hard, especially when the testimony appears to suggest some confusion of thought, some incompatibility with itself or with known fact elsewhere. He may perhaps find it necessary to say something like "Do you *really* mean what you appear to be saying?"

But he will lose all professional respectability if he forgets that he is only there to elicit reliable and lucid testimony, not to determine its content. He must not usurp the witness's function. He has no competence to do so, no authority: he wasn't there.

Chapter Three

Let us now look a little more closely at the concept of intellectual freedom, primarily as it concerns the academic person.

Nobody supposes that those who undertake teaching and research in the university, or the intelligentsia in general, ought to be given special privileges as citizens. But there is a general moral consensus—to which I assent fully—that they must be subject to no outside pressure as regards the substance of what they discover and teach. Some interesting questions are raised by the basis and implications of this consensus: it seems to depend crucially, for example, upon a definite faith in objective and ascertainable truth, such as is hardly compatible with certain existential and other scepticisms of the day. (If truth cannot be actually apprehended in some measure, the search for it becomes absurd rather than sacred.) But for the present, we can leave all such questions to one side and agree that the government (or any comparable agency) acts wickedly if it intrudes upon the scholar or scientist or thinker in any field in order to prevent him from reaching—or perhaps from publicising—unwelcome findings. He must be free to follow truth, no matter where it leads him—even if it leads him to conclusions which are highly embarrassing to those in power. "Freedom of speech" can never be total: in my view at least, obscenity and libel can be subjected to legal restraint without injustice. But any censorship of thought and ideas is an abomination.

People sometimes express this principle, rather inaccurately, by saying that a man is entitled to believe—and therefore to say—whatever he likes. As against the State, he is. But as before God and his conscience, he sins grievously if he literally believes *what he likes*—that is, if he allows personal preference to govern his beliefs. We all have a basic duty of living mentally in the real world to the best of our ability—of accepting reality or the facts (which can often be unpleasant) in preference to our own fantasies and desires (which will usually be comforting). This might be called a duty of intellectual chastity: it is dishonest and wrong to grant admission to every wandering and irresponsible belief, merely because of its attractiveness, its short-term allure. Here, as with the other sort of chastity, freedom from external control needs to be distinguished from mere self-indulgent permissiveness.

All freedoms impose responsibilities, and are discredited by any neglect or betrayal of these. Intellectual freedom is rightly given to the scholar or scientist or other thinker, and it imposes a particular responsibility upon him: he needs to be free from outside pressure, precisely so as to be totally obedient to the objective and determinate nature of his subject-matter. He must be under the least possible temptation to falsify this, by misrepresentation or distortion or even by silence.

Governmental threats and promises can obviously tempt him to falsify his subject-matter in such ways. It may be as well to remember that other factors can do so too. Inordinate attachment to his own most cherished hypothesis can certainly do so; or ambition; or that most corrupting thing, the desire to be fashionable and with the trend.

The main thing is that any such temptation must be kept to the minimum, and resisted wherever it is inescapably encountered. This goes for any kind of scholar or thinker, no matter what his field. Any falsification of his subject-matter will be a sin against the academic code of honour, whatever further consequences it may have at other levels.

There are many obvious senses in which the life and work of the Catholic theologian resemble the life and work of the academic or researcher in any other field. He undergoes his long training, he earns his degrees, he secures his possibly tenured post: he moves from his private office to the library and then to the lecture-room: he stimulates or bores his pupils as the case may be: he writes and publishes, he becomes embroiled in arguments which may sometimes be acrimonious, he may possibly achieve fame and influence in the larger world. And all the time, like any other academic or researcher, he must enjoy complete academic or intellectual freedom: that is to say, he must live and work and think and write in complete docile obedience to his subject-matter, and must be protected as far as possible from any external or internal temptation to falsify this.

As we have seen, the subject-matter which gave him something definite to talk about and a verification-method for use in connection with it—and which was thus the whole basis of his academic respectability—has to be defined in some such words as "the Catholic Faith" or "the mind of the Church": that is what he must not falsify. But the distinctive nature of his subject-matter and his verification-method means that his life and work are in some respects rather different from the life and work of other academics and researchers, and on lines which—if he has any of that intellectual pride which is the characteristic disease of clever people—he may find irksome. The temptation to falsify, which can come upon any scholar or thinker, may therefore come upon him in distinctive ways.

In the first place, when he compares himself with his colleagues in other fields, he may find it irksome that he cannot hope to make amazing new discoveries except in certain very limited senses.

A university will commonly define its research-function in terms of the "extension of knowledge"; and when we attach high value to intellectual or academic freedom, we do so with "truth" in mind but also "the search for truth". Any such extension or search can be imagined as a lateral or horizontal movement, an exploration and conquest of new territories, within which many great surprises will doubtlessly await discovery: thus Fleming became famous for discovering penicillin and Ventris for deciphering Linear B, and every young scholar or scientist can dream of similar glory. But the Catholic Faith defines itself as a *fides semel sanctis tradita*, a public revelation made once and for all nearly two thousand years ago, capable of "development" in Newman's rather technical sense (as when a lawyer interrogates a witness) but not otherwise capable of being augmented by radically new discoveries. A great theologian's researches will substantially deepen our understanding of it while also assisting that process of "development", but only by what we must imagine as a vertical movement or process within already-known territory. The nature of his subject–matter rules out any lateral exploration and discovery and indeed every kind of radical novelty: he cannot hope for the ecstasy of the scholar or scientist who suddenly finds good grounds for saying "All my predecessors were wrong! In this important matter, the truth was never perceived at all until *I* unearthed it!"

Any Catholic theologian who thought and spoke like that, in a matter of central importance to the Faith, would be cutting the ground from under his own academic feet.

This does not mean that he is confined to the mere repetitious singing of old songs to familiar tunes. He *can* be a pioneer, but only in certain ways: he can make some great discovery, but this will need to take one of three possible forms. It may be a re-discovery of something that was always there in the Faith but had been under-developed or overlooked or perhaps just given insufficient emphasis, for historical reasons that may well be ascertainable. Then, it may be a useful casting of the old light upon new situations and discoveries, and there will always be plenty of these; and finally it may itself be a genuine

discovery, but in method rather than in substance. The most spectacular example here is St. Thomas's amazing discovery—it seemed absurd to some good Catholics at the time—that the truths of Christian faith could be fruitfully handled and explored, without loss or damage, by the methods of the pagan Aristotle. Further discoveries of the same kind may well be made in the future: there is a least some scope here for theological ambition. (There are also continuous possibilities of giving radically new *imaginative* expression to the old Faith. But these are open to the literary man as such, rather than to the theologian in his academic capacity: I mention them with C. S. Lewis and G. K. Chesterton in mind, and neither of these was a theologian.)

If certain people dislike this idea of a once-and-for-all "deposit of faith" and prefer to speak of "on-going revelation", it needs no great cynicism to see why they desire this particular falsification of the Catholic theologian's subject-matter It offers him a kind of innovatory scope, available to scholars in other fields but necessarily not to him.

In the second place, he lives in a peculiarly intimate relationship with his subject-matter: he needs to live it as well as to become erudite about it.

In this he is not wholly unique. A medical scientist needs to look after his own health, the Professor of Law will be in trouble if he does not obey the law as well as studying it. But neither the health of the one nor the virtuous behaviour of the other will contribute directly to the understanding of his subject-matter; whereas the theologian will not fully *see* his subject-matter unless he brings the light of faith, prayer, and humility to bear upon it. Without that light, he will not—in the fullest sense—"know" what he is talking about.

Let us imagine a man born deaf, who has never heard a note of music in his life. It is conceivable (though unlikely) that he might embark upon the study of music, even so: he could read all the books, and become (in a sense) very well-informed about it. Stretching our credulity to the breaking-point, we can say that there is nothing to prevent him from becoming Professor of Music—just as an atheist, or some nominally religious man without an actual breath of faith or prayer or humility in his whole body, might (in theory) become Professor of Theology. But in no such case would the professor really "know" what he was talking about.

Less extreme cases do occur in fact. It is no rare thing to meet an atheist or agnostic upon whom

Catholicism exerts a kind of fascination, so that he becomes extremely well-informed about every aspect and element of it and wants to discuss it all the time. It is a curious experience to talk to such a man as from within the Faith. He knows about everything and understands nothing: he is like that deaf musicologist.

It is necessary, but it is not sufficient, for the theologian to be a learned man. He also needs to lead the life of Christ in some measure, the life of the Church, in certain respects especially. His theology, and therefore his academic respectability, will not necessarily suffer much direct damage from the fact that he keeps a mistress. But it will suffer a great deal of damage if he habitually commits the greater sin of intellectual pride.

In the third place, while Catholic theology becomes academically respectable by reason of having an appropriate verification-method—without which any discipline must be no more than a matter of personal experience and opinion—it has a verification-method which can sometimes be tiresomely slow. New hypotheses may be formulated very freely in any field; and in some fields, they can be verified or falsified very quickly. This is pleasant for the scholar or scientist in question, since it is only human to desire high-speed recognition and acceptance for one's thinking, and therefore an early chance of correcting it where necessary. But any hypothesis in Catholic theology can only be verified or falsified by a process of testing against the mind of the Church; and while this can be an almost instantaneous process in certain clear-cut cases, it may take decades or generations.

In the meantime, the hypothesis or speculation in question remains exactly that, a hypothesis or speculation: it will be an academic impropriety to trumpet it forth to the world as though it had some higher standing—the standing, perhaps, of a spectacular and fully verified discovery in science or scholarship. The Pope has emphasised this principle from the Church's angle in the Apostolic Constitution *Sapientia Christiana* (1979): it needs equal emphasis from the purely academic or intellectual angle.

Any such premature trumpeting-forth will also be irresponsible and unkind. Consider cancer-research. It is the heartless practice of the media to announce each tiny new discovery in that field as though it were a major and decisive break-through—as though the hateful disease were on the brink of being conquered completely. This makes for a good news-story, but also for a cruel raising of false or premature hopes. It has been the

analogously harmful practice of the media, during the 1960s and 1970s, to announce every new hypothesis or speculation in Catholic theology—especially when of some radical or disruptive sort and therefore more newsworthy—as though it possessed immediate and definitive certainty and so rendered everything else obsolete and absurd. This was unrealistic in itself: it fostered the curious illusion that the most "important" theologians of the day were those most manifestly in conflict with the mind of the Church and so with the only possible basis for their own theology.

It was also psychologically damaging to many people. There are some fields in which the exploratory thinker or researcher carries a measure of public responsibility: the current anxieties about recombinant DNA provide us with one instance of this, and Catholic theology provides us—very definitely—with another. It is an academic discipline, but it is not *only* that: its practitioner needs to remember that he also has a kind of pastoral responsibility towards his less erudite fellow-Catholics and others too, especially but not only if he is a priest. He can explore freely. But charity and justice require him to be careful about what he says and how he says it.

An analogy is provided here by the thing which —in our non-religious experience—comes closest to what we call "faith": namely, married love and trust. Let us imagine that we know a married man who loves and trusts his wife; and let us now use our intellectual freedom in order to raise the question of whether she is faithful to him or not. This is a real question, capable of a clear-cut answer: how shall we answer it? If we desire to proceed on some rigorously intellectual basis, we shall probably have to admit that we don't know: inescapably cogent evidence, one way or the other, is simply not available. In a situation of this kind, should we therefore talk loudly as though the question were entirely open? Does intellectual integrity oblige us to talk to this husband as though his wife were as likely as not to be a whore?

It does not: we have no such excuse for committing the sin of Iago and sowing the seeds of doubt in his mind. Even if we came across some evidence suggesting that his wife might possibly be unfaithful in fact, we would still need to think twice or a thousand times before mentioning the fact to him.

Disturbing and otherwise unwelcome truths do sometimes need to be proclaimed, but always responsibly: intellectual freedom cannot decently be understood as exempting the enquirer from the common decencies and responsibilities of speech and social relationship. This fact, and that analogy of the husband and wife, should be borne in mind when some maverick theologian gets rebuked by Rome for "disturbing the minds of the faithful". This kind of rebuke comes in for much scorn: "I see—so the simple faithful must be wrapped in cotton-wool and prevented from hearing anything that might upset them and even (oh horror!) start them *thinking* on their own account! Is that what you want?" Such sneers would be well-merited if the Catholic faith were a field of academic enquiry and nothing else, having no crucial involvement in the lives of people at large; which is not the case, except within the enquirer's ivory tower. In the larger world, it resembles married love in being enormously important and also in being extremely vulnerable to irresponsible chatter.

We can hardly expect theological speculation to be kept secret until fully verified against the mind of the Church over some long period. Any such proposal would require us to understand "the mind of the Church", for this purpose, in the most narrowly ecclesiastical and Roman sense alone, and would be unpractical even so: the news would be bound to leak out. But the Catholic theologian therefore carries an obligation which is not shared by all of his academic colleagues. His responsibility for others, as well as his concern for his own intellectual propriety, obliges him to make it as clear as possible—if necessary, loudly and in public—that his untested speculations are not to be taken as certain and over-riding truth in transcendental matters. That isn't something which he is competent to offer.

Nor, individually, are you and I. If we are asked to express an opinion for or against some new line in theological speculation, it will often be a very good reply to say "Ask me again in a hundred years' time".

In the fourth place—shocking though this may seem to some—that long delay won't matter very much. No possible new development in theology is of any great practical importance for the Christian: at the best, it will be nowhere near as important as its proponents will be likely— in our high-speed century—to suppose. Unlike science, this is a field in which very old books are, on the whole, more likely to be useful than very new books.

Let me here compare the theologian with a professional man rather than some other kind of academic—with a doctor, perhaps, or a lawyer. The average citizen may well take an interest in the latest findings of scholarly and scientific research, but he has no real need to do so: he can ignore them completely and still struggle on through life more or less successfully, more or less happily, as most people do in fact. It is otherwise with those two learned professions. I very much want my doctor to keep up-to-date with the latest developments in medicine: otherwise, I may fail to get the benefit of some new discovery in diagnosis or treatment. For similar reasons, I want my lawyer to keep up-to-date with the latest statutes and decisions, so that he can help me to dodge round them.

But I have no parallel need in respect of the theologian. His also is a learned profession: it concerns man as an immortal soul, as medicine concerns man as a living body and law as a social animal. But these two are evolving or expanding fields of knowledge, in a sense in which theology is not: novelty or up-to-dateness thus has a practical urgency in those first two fields which it lacks in the third. There, we can afford to wait.

I do not wish to be misunderstood: I am not trying to cut the theologian, or even the speculative or innovative theologian, down to size in any absolute way, as though his studies were valueless. All studies are valuable, since knowledge is in general better than ignorance. But academic studies differ considerably in their immediately practical importance for mankind. We may say that the Church (meaning ourselves) has two tasks, or that its single task has two aspects: we have to be concerned with the salvation of souls in the next world, and with the establishment of the Kingdom in this one. Various things hold us back from the completion of this task or these tasks, pride or self-love outstandingly: what gets no support from faith—or from spirituality, or from experience—is any attribution of crucial importance, as regards that task or those tasks, to theological novelty or up-to-dateness.

A partial exception can be made in respect of the theologian's work as conceptual translator. If the Gospel fails to get across in our time, this is—to a certain extent—because people literally don't understand what the Church is trying to tell them. It therefore becomes very important that we should re-state the ancient Faith, as far as possible, in the language of modern man. This cannot be done completely, since "the language of modern man" is mostly that of a secular, scientific, and positivist culture, and is semantically incapable of carrying deep religious meaning. In a highly relevant sense of the Lord's words, not everybody has "ears to hear": the evangelical task thus includes a difficult and burdensome element of linguistic education and indeed of linguistic liberation.

This is an urgent task and it needs to be done mostly by theologians. But it is not strictly theological work, even so: it concerns the expression rather than the substance of faith, and stands in relation to the Church rather as a translator stands in relation to an author.

The translator's great danger is that of intruding his own ideas into the text before him and so falsifying this. It's one thing to re-state the ancient Faith, as far as possible, in the language of modern man: it's quite another thing to select from the ancient Faith those elements which are favoured by oneself and deemed easily acceptable to modern man, modifying or playing down the remainder.

This distinction is of great topical importance. The area in which new theological work can claim the greatest urgency is also the area in which it is most liable to intellectual self-destruction.

In the fifth place, the Catholic theologian is almost unique among academics in that he does not speak simply and solely for himself, since what he claims to expound and interpret and develop has to be "the mind of the Church" if his title is to have any accuracy. And while he is certainly part of the Church, neither he as an individual nor any consensus of his professional colleagues can be simply equated with it.

We might express this by saying that he differs from most other academics in that his subject-matter is alive and can talk back at him, and even correct him if necessary.

In this he is enviable. How often the historian must curse the stubborn silence of his documents, which tell him many things but not the maddeningly elusive thing which he wants to know! How pleased the physicist would be, if he could beckon to some passing neutron and ask it to give him a full first-hand account of its activities and movements, its hopes and fears, its colourful sex-life! But most such kinds of subject-matter are dead and don't talk. With the more ignoble part of the scholar's or scientist's mind, he may be rather glad of this: it saves him from much danger of being embarrassingly corrected. But in his more ideal capacity, as a disinterested seeker after truth, he ought to welcome any such enlightening correction if only it were available.

To the Catholic theologian, it is available. In a way, he resembles not a historian or physicist but a student of contemporary affairs. If such a student writes a book about recent political developments, he will naturally come under the judgment of his academic peers as regards the quality of his work. But he will also come under the judgment of the politicians in question as regards the fidelity with which he has recorded and interpreted their views, their motivations, their behaviour. His subject-matter can talk back at him.

It will not always be with perfect honesty that

politicians do so: such people commonly dislike any telling of the full truth about them. But the premise which gave academic respectability to the Catholic theologian also—and in the same breath—gave him an automatic assurance that when the Church talks back at him in formally definitive terms, it will do so reliably. It will be correcting his mistakes: it will be helping his work along, not interfering with it in any obstructive or restrictive way.

It is therefore a profound mistake—although a very common one—to pity the poor Catholic theologian because his tyrannical Church denies him full freedom of thought and expression. His condition is no worse than that of his colleagues in other fields. They also lack perfect autonomy or freedom of the mind: they also are morally tied down in obedience to whatever their subject-matter may tell them, with whatever voice—living or dead—is characteristic of this field or that. The historian is the slave of source-documents, the scientist of experimental findings. Such things can and must be tested for authenticity, since their appearance may be deceptive: the document may be a forgery, the conditions of an experiment may have been imperfectly controlled. In much the same way, something previously considered to represent "the mind of the

Church" will sometimes turn out to be a merely human opinion, held by many people who were in the Church.

But in so far as such doubts are eliminated in the appropriate way—that is, by a further and more searching interrogation of the subject-matter—a duty of acceptance or obedience follows; and this will be the consummation, not the denial, of academic freedom.

There are only two absolute freedoms of the mind, and the university and the intellectual community at large must try to eliminate both. They are the freedoms of ignorance and of dishonesty.

From what I have been saying, certain consequences follow, such as have their moral importance for anyone who accepts office—especially *paid* office—as a teacher of the Catholic religion and an enquirer into its richer depths, in the university or the school or the Church generally.

I will introduce the first of these by an anecdote, telling this in the words of the late Douglas Woodruff.

The French Directory in 1797 wanted to get Sebastien Mercier, a survival from both the Girondin and the Robespierre days, out of politics, where he was an embarrassment, and so they made him

Professor of History at Paris. He accepted the Chair; but from it he promptly started to teach that the earth was flat. He added that the sun revolved round it; and Copernicus and Newton, said he, were rogues and fools, who had been altogether too successful in making people disbelieve their own eyes. If people objected that the flatness of the earth was geography, not history, he had his answer that the roguery of astronomers was history, and important history at that.[1]

I do not know how accurately that story is there told, or how it ended: much may have depended upon whether Professor Mercier had tenure or not. But if he did indeed persist in acting as there indicated, he would have suffered no injustice—no intrusion upon his academic freedom—if the University had brought disciplinary pressure to bear upon him in due course. It is simply dishonest to accept money for doing some specific job or supplying some specific commodity, and then to do or supply something different. Your views on the flatness of this earth, however challenging in themselves, are not what you are paid to supply as Professor of History; and if you are paid to teach people the Catholic Faith, mere commercial honesty decrees that you must do

[1] Douglas Woodruff, *More Talking at Random* (London: Burnes Oates, 1944).

precisely that, and not something else preferred by yourself.

This is a moral issue about which we laymen are entitled to have strong feelings, where clerical behaviour is concerned. Let us not forget that all these great Catholic institutions which we see around us were built and are now maintained, ultimately, by the pennies of the poor—occasionally by the millions of the rich—and that economically speaking, the entire ecclesiastical institution is wholly parasitical upon the laity. I do not mind this in the least; nor do I consider it desirable or even possible that those who thus pay the ecclesiastical piper should call the doctrinal and moral tune. But it is morally outrageous when money raised from the people (mostly from poor people) for one definable purpose is converted without their consent to another and radically different purpose; and this happens very often in the Church of today.

The question arises in a number of versions, but most conspicuously in connection with appointments to teaching or preaching positions. Let us suppose (for example) that some college or university appoints some man to its Chair of Catholic Theology, knowing perfectly well that his mind is miles and miles away from the mind of the Church. As between the university and this new Professor, so long as no further parties are involved, there is no danger of dishonesty: both parties enter into the deal with their eyes open. But further parties usually will be involved. Professors seldom work wholly in secret: they mostly give lectures and publish books. They put their wares on offer in the world's intellectual marketplace.

Now in England we have something called the Trade Descriptions Act, and it affects all those who put ordinary commercial wares on offer. It obliges you to label them with at least something like honesty and accuracy. The most ardent devotee of the free market can hardly object to the principle that if you label and promote your wares deceptively, public authority can properly intervene. It will not then be interfering with the free market, but only making sure that the market really *is* free. In so far as the customer is bemused by deceptive labelling or promotion, he is un-free, hog-tied in delusion by some smart operator with his own axe to grind.

Caveat emptor, they say: let the purchaser be careful in his own interest. But the sad fact is that not all of us are capable of analysing and evaluating the many complex products which we find pressed upon us.

Something similar is true of the commerce in beliefs. In the marketplace of these last fifteen years, many things have been packaged and labelled

and very insistently sold as Catholic theologies
of some "new", or "progressive", or "liberal"
sort, when on any objective reckoning they were
more or less radical departures from Catholic
Christianity as such. When anything of that kind
happens, the Church can surely invoke the pro-
visions of the Faith Descriptions Act in order to
save the customer from being fooled.

But I would prefer—at this point—to put the
emphasis elsewhere, appealing to the values of
the university rather than to those of the Church.

I regard academic and intellectual freedom as
an extremely important value. But it does impose
its obligations and carry its dangers, as all other
freedoms do. I have mentioned the obligation of
integrity which it imposes upon the scholar: he
must not dogmatise beyond his competence, and
he must never allow any public confusion to arise
as between unconfirmed hypothesis or speculation
on the one hand, and on the other, any kind of
substantially confirmed or verified knowledge.

The corresponding danger is a real one. People
are hungry for certainty, and are frequently all
too willing to believe the "expert" as such, far
beyond the limited field of his actual *expertise*; and
it will not always be easy for him to resist the
temptation involved in such flattery. Our inborn
pride tempts us all to see our mere opinions or

speculations as total and indeed obvious truth: a rigorous training of the mind, such as a university should provide, will reduce this danger but not always with complete success, since it is a moral and not merely an intellectual danger. And it will be all the more serious if the opinions and speculations in question are popular and fashionable and congenial to ourselves, appear to be on the winning side, and tie in closely with what seems to be the wave of the new exciting future. Too easily, we shall then be able to forget that they still need rigorous testing: we shall be disposed to treat them as instant certainties.

Such dangers are particularly serious for the Catholic theologian, who operates in a battlefield rather than an ivory tower. The following of Christ, easy in one sense, is tremendously exacting in another: there is therefore a steady, fierce, and intellectually uncritical demand for any kind of new thinking that will ease the pain of it, enabling people to have it both ways—to remain Catholics in some Pickwickian sense, while not being held to the knife-edge (or Cross) of what Catholic or integral Christianity actually means. No such compromise is in fact possible: "He that is not with me is against me." But there will be heavy strain upon the integrity and the intellectual humility of any scholar whose work appears to suggest otherwise, and not only because his books will sell widely on a somewhat false basis. People will want to make him into a prophet: they will also want to make him into a martyr, and will eagerly see as his martyrdom some course of events which—when seen in detachment and more soberly—is totally without that kind of awfulness, that kind of glamour.

In my experience, which is limited but real, first-class scholars and scientists tend to be humble men. There are exceptions, and I have known one or two gross exceptions. But most such men are intellectually cautious, and would prefer to see their favourite hypotheses put to the test for another generation or two, rather than seeing them proclaimed prematurely as eternal certainties. (Their motives here need not always be of the highest sort. A premature claim to certainty is intellectually improper. But it also exposes one to the danger of a humiliating comeuppance, such as one would prefer to avoid.)

Catholic theologians, being Christians by definition, ought to display this kind of patient humility to an exceptional degree. It seems to me that most of them do. But they are only human, and some of them are clearly at risk: there is no more powerful solvent of wisdom and prudence and faith itself than intellectual pride, especially when reinforced by the applause of the crowd and the heady delights offered by false versions of the martyr's role.

To a man thus intoxicated, a sobering reminder of the intellect's limitations will be a great kindness —a safeguarding of the academic respectability which he is in danger of losing, not an intrusion upon it. But he may resent any such reminder none the less, since if taken seriously, it would cost him his shock-value. He would not hit the headlines any more.

It is always pleasant, in a way, to hit the headlines. The astronomer—or, for that matter, the historian—who wishes to do so can always follow the example of Sebastien Mercier and tell us all, loudly and with great assurance, that the earth is flat. The media will adore him.

Chapter Four

It is always disagreeable to find oneself fixed, inescapably, in any position of subordination and restraint. A Christian, remembering the Gospel, will try not to resent any such situation too deeply: it offers him spiritual benefit, whereas there is spiritual danger in being on top of the heap and wholly one's own master. But this latter situation, however dangerous, is what our pride will always prefer.

This moral issue is a painful one; and it will be good news, therefore, if it turns out not to arise in some area where it appears to arise.

It can appear to arise for any Catholic who lives and works in the secular university or the intellectual world generally. He can there seem to lack an autonomy and freedom which others enjoy. These others will sometimes tease him about it, perhaps with heavy irony. "Oh, I'm sorry, I forgot. You're one of these Catholics, aren't you? You have to toe the ecclesiastical line, you have to ask the Pope's permission before you're allowed to concede that two and two make four; and if the Pope says that two and two make seventeen, then that's how it's got to be for you. How truly inspirational it is, in this sceptical age, to encounter such faith! How deeply you are envied by us poor agnostics, suffering under the cruel limitation of needing only to say what we actually believe to be true!" And so forth.

Such wisecracks can indeed make a Catholic feel like a second-class citizen of the intellectual world, hog-tied, not his own master, unable to enjoy that world's full freedom except in defiance of Church authority and at the cost of his orthodoxy in the Faith.

What I have been trying to suggest is that all such feelings are illusory, generated by purely accidental factors of the historical and psychological kind, and in particular, by the very widespread tendency to interpret faith in political categories, to confuse truth with power. If there is no revelation of God, then the Catholics are of course simply wrong. But if there is such a revelation, then fidelity to the substance of this is no more a deprivation of freedom than is fidelity to the facts or the data in any other field. We are not second-class citizens: we are no worse off than anybody else.

None the less, those feelings of subordination and restraint—however irrational—can be powerful, and can then prompt the theologian to actions of which the intellectually suicidal nature will not initially be apparent to himself.

This danger arises because in our kind of society, Western and liberal and secular, academic people and the intelligentsia in general exercise a kind of priestly office, a social role of leadership and guidance, in respect of which they are totally autonomous, recognising no authority higher than their own. Where most kinds of subject-matter are concerned, this is a wholly desirable state of affairs: the tendency of governments—especially when totalitarian—to intrude upon this autonomy of theirs is what makes us all so rightly sensitive to the whole question of academic and intellectual freedom. But when the Catholic theologian attempts to assume his own version of this social priesthood, this autonomy, he finds another priesthood already in possession, and one which will often be represented—locally at least—by men less clever than himself, who will none the less claim over-riding authority over him in those transcendental matters of faith and morals which are his professional concern.

If he is proud and hasty by temperament and has forgotten the basis upon which he was—

against certain objections—admitted to the academic community, he may then feel exasperated; he may come to imagine that there is a real conflict between his Catholic orthodoxy and his intellectual freedom—as though what I have called "the mind of the Church", as expressed upon occasion by Rome, were as arbitrarily and externally tyrannical as the will of the Kremlin.

In fact, as I have tried to show, it was only the mind of the Church that gave his intellectual freedom anything to work on—any subject-matter, any verification-method, any academic respectability. Lacking that, his intellectual powers, however freely exercised, could hardly take him beyond simple theism, if indeed they took him as far as that. (They don't always take able thinkers that far.) Any supposedly Catholic theology which ignores or contradicts the mind of the Church is self-destructive: it is bound to work out as a vaguely theistic scepticism at the best, and at the worst, an exercise in unsupported dogmatism and therefore a great intellectual impropriety. The logic of the matter shows that it must be so: the present-day scene shows that it is so in fact. But the message has not been universally grasped: it's an unwelcome one for those who prefer the appearance of autonomy to intellectual coherence.

With these considerations in mind, I propose to consider a conspicuous phenomenon of our time.

The years since the Second Vatican Council have shown us, within the Catholic Church, a development which—although it has much precedent—seems wonderfully new to some and outrageously new to others. I find it a rather embarrassing thing to discuss with the people concerned, since they tempt me strongly to see their position and talk about it in psychological and *ad hominem* terms, which is always bad manners. But it is crucial for my subject and needs candid treatment.

What I have in mind is not a development of the Church as a whole: it is a minority-thing, characteristic of middle-class Catholic intellectuals, clerical and lay, in the white-skinned countries of the affluent West—notably in Holland, France, Canada, and the United States, though elsewhere (my own country included) in varying but lesser degrees. It arouses little support among aristocrats or working-class people, or among the dark-skinned Catholics of the Third World: it exists in Latin America, but there with political complications which are irrelevant to my present subject. If, in general, it looks bigger and more universal than it is, this is largely because those who are in a position to make themselves heard influentially and in public—such as writers, editors, publishers, educators in school or university, ecclesiastical bureaucrats, and so forth—have obvious reasons for favouring it.

Although this partially new development is so largely an affair of the intelligentsia, it would be insufficient to see it in primarily doctrinal terms, as an intellectually definable position that might be debated on its merits. It has that character to some degree, but it is much more conspicuously a state of mind. The most obvious thing about the people in question—and this is where I necessarily turn psychological and *ad hominem*—is that they are in a state of unresolved inner conflict about the Catholic Faith. They claim the Catholic name, and even the Roman Catholic name, firmly and (if their right to it is challenged) even fiercely: yet they persist in saying things which are more or less flatly in contradiction with what all men, believers and atheists alike, recognise as the characteristic faith and morals of the Roman Catholic Church. To their own satisfaction at least, they resolve this contradiction by claiming to be the pioneers, the vanguard of that great renewal to which the Second Vatican Council undoubtedly called the Church: if you point out the numerous points at which the Council explicitly repudiated their way of thinking, they usually appeal from the letter to the alleged "spirit" of the Council. It is crucial for them that in respect of faith and morals, the word "Catholic" should recently have acquired a new and total elasticity of meaning, and that the Council—as seen mythologically rather than factually—should have somehow authorised and initiated a discontinuity with the Catholic past which is 100 percent in principle, and in practice—with one important qualification—just what the individual chooses to make of it.

The important qualification is that the individual must make *something* of that discontinuity, and something fairly substantial. If he chooses to see it only as a minor re-styling of the package, the old Product remaining what it always was and always must be, he will be in trouble. Terrible words will be hurled at him: conservative, Tridentine, ultramontane, and (worst of all) pre-Conciliar.

It is my instinct, at least, to see this development in primarily psychological terms. Anyone with a poor command of language can naturally talk in a confused and contradictory manner. But in highly-educated and articulate people, self-contradiction will usually be an indication of personal stress; and this is what I see, first of all, in those who are desperate to find some way of being a Catholic without actually being a Catholic

—in those who will say to you "I am a Catholic, of course, but . . .", following that initial statement with something that contradicts it more or less flatly.

But the matter can be seen in many other ways as well. There is certainly a great deal of sex to this development: that is, any discussion of the relevant questions shows a strong tendency to come back in a somewhat obsessive manner to *Humanae Vitae*, and to sexual morality in general, before very long. Although few will admit it, this is clearly the heart of the matter for some: I have met any number of people who considered any more traditional or authentic Catholicism to be sufficiently refuted—on *reductio ad absurdum* lines —by the fact that if accepted, it would entail an acceptance of that encyclical, that teaching. The manifest rightness of contraception—which all Christendom regarded as a manifest obscenity and sin until very recently, and to which Freud attached "the dishonourable name of perversion"— thus becomes almost the primary axiom of a radically new ecclesiology, a radically new notion of where the mind of the Church is to be found.

If I were treating this subject at length, I would indeed lay great emphasis upon this sexual aspect of the matter, as arising in affluent consumer-societies whose instinct it is to attach primary importance to the immediate gratification of felt desires. (The contraceptive has much in common with the credit-card: both are methods of implementing the principle "I want: therefore I am entitled to have, and *now*".) But the phenomenon does have other aspects.

Some have seen it as a phenomenon of capitalism in decline: Pope John Paul II exemplifies its weakness behind the Iron Curtain, and it does tend to follow the private-enterprise principle of modifying the product as necessary in order to meet consumer-demand—of telling people what they want to hear, rather than what they need to know, which was neither the practice nor the precept of the Lord Jesus. In ecclesiastical terms, it seems like an attempt to make the Catholic Church more like the Church of England, which hardly claims to know what it's talking about and so leaves its members in a state which might be called doctrinal freedom but which might also be called doctrinal nihilism. Theologically, it has a strong flavour of Gnosticism: its vocabulary is full of words like "meaning", "intuition", "experience", "sensitivity", "awareness", and other rough translations of *gnosis*. Philosophically, it tends to a radical scepticism. Where it rejects the dogmatic utterances of the Church, it usually does so not on some ground of their falsity, so much as from a suspicion or conviction that doctrines are merely verbalisations of the current experience of the believing community—whatever "believing" may mean in such a context—and cannot ever be true *or* false in any more permanent and objective sense. (But this radical scepticism can co-exist with an extremely confident sort of dogmatism. Earlier on, I mentioned three questions of the transcendental kind: the question of whether women can become priests; that question of contraception and *Humanae Vitae*; and the question of which developments, in the Church's recent history, are to be seen as the work of the Holy Spirit. A sceptic or rationalist might declare all three to be unanswerable when stated in fully transcendental terms: the man whom I shall rather provocatively call the neo-Modernist answers all three—and many others like them—with total confidence, as though on the basis of some more-than-papal infallibility, and in flat contradiction of Catholic tradition.)

I am disposed to attach great importance to a political and sociological interpretation of this phenomenon. It is democratic in theory but not in practice: it suggests the situation which prevails in some communist society, where an ancient monarchy has been rejected and where power— nominally held by the people—is in fact jealously retained by the self-appointed Party élite. Within the Church, in fact, we are now witnessing a kind of take-over bid—an attempt, on the part of a self-appointed intellectual élite, to gain power at the expense of the Apostolic Hierarchy on the one hand and the common people on the other. I have often observed that in the people concerned —who characteristically talk in the language of democracy, often of the political Left, even of Marxism—their hatred of the episcopal and papal *magisterium* can be fully equalled by their contempt for the old folk-Catholicism of the poor and the popular devotions and loyalties associated with it. About all that, they speak as nobody nowadays would dare to speak about—say—popular Hinduism: they represent what is perhaps the last flowering of the arrogantly colonialising mentality, in all its confidence of superiority over the poor ignorant savages.

It will have been observed that I look upon this development with a certain detachment, and even critically. If I were a better Christian than I am, it would be my instinct to look upon it only with compassion. An unresolved internal conflict can be a painful thing: we should be slow to pass judgment upon those who are tormented by the impossibility of following the Lord in the wholeness or completeness (*kata holos*, from which we get "Catholic") of faith, but strictly on one's own terms or on terms congenial to the dominant secular thought of one's time, and with the full right of picking and choosing (*hairesis*, from which we get "heresy").

But while any personal judgment needs to be extremely cautious, the facts need to be faced. It seems clear (in many cases at least) that the people concerned have more or less lost the Faith, are naturally unwilling to face the fact of this loss, and are therefore passionately desirous to believe —at any cost in plausibility—that Catholic Christianity is somehow evolving and *must* evolve into something in which they still do believe; which can be a liberal Protestantism in one case, a vague pan-Anglicanism in another, and a secular welfare-state humanism (with Marxist seasoning added according to taste) in a third. Their words seem to me to rule out any alternative interpretation.

Now, as the post-Conciliar dust settles, it is becoming increasingly obvious that Catholicism is not so evolving, was never intended to do so by the Council, and in fact *cannot* do so.

The neo-Modernist may therefore find himself driven by logic and realism to a painful choice. "He that is not with me is against me."

For my present purposes, I want to concentrate upon one particular aspect of this movement or tendency within the Church. It has often been criticised from the orthodox Catholic standpoint: I want to raise the question of what it looks like when considered in more simply academic or intellectual terms, and even in sceptical terms.

There is a certain sense in which it appears to favour the interests of the academic and intellectual community, or of its Catholic members at least: it wants these to prevail in the Church, or at least to achieve such a degree of autonomy that they will no longer feel like second-class citizens. As I have observed, it can be seen as an effort or bid in that sense.

My concern is with the self-destructive nature of any such aspiration, when considered in the light of various considerations which have already been mentioned in this essay.

Neo-Modernism is not primarily a positive doctrinal position. But in so far as it can be stated doctrinally, it is above all a rejection of the belief —expressed as firmly by Vatican II as by any other manifestation of the Catholic mind—that the Church's teaching office or *magisterium*, although widely diffused in various senses, is exercised primarily and definitively by the Catholic bishops, defined as such by their unity with the See of Peter, and teaching not by virtue of the intellectual powers which they may or may not possess, but by virtue of a divine *charisma* which they acquire as successors of the Apostles.

What takes the place of this *magisterium*, for the neo-Modernist, is in some ways rather like that "private judgment" to which supremacy was given in some versions of Protestantism. But it is very much not the "private judgment" of the possibly unlettered individual to whom the Spirit speaks inwardly as he cons the Good Book: it is very much the judgment of certain intelligent and learned people, speaking as such and with no further authority or qualification apart from their conformity to certain currently fashionable patterns of thought. In the Church which the neo-Modernist desires to see, the pope and the bishops will still be tolerated and allowed to put forward their points of view. But these will always be subject to higher judgment, and not—as in the Gallican view of things—to the higher judgment of the Church as a whole: the theologians and other intellectuals of correct liberal orientation, although a small and unrepresentative minority, will act as a kind of Supreme Court, invoking their superior *magisterium* and telling us whether to accept or reject the formally-defined teaching of bishops and councils and popes, both ancient and modern.

Even in matters of faith and morals, therefore,

the Church will become a charientocracy: its intellectuals and experts, operating as such, will and indeed *should* call the shots. This view of things became very apparent at the time of *Humanae Vitae*. A committee of intellectuals and experts had been appointed by one pope and continued by another to consider that question of contraception; and many people were outraged when Paul VI had the effrontery to disregard and even contradict its findings, just as though his was the superior *magisterium*. And to make matters worse, it seemed that he had not "proved his case" with anything like sufficient cogency—as though it were his job, as Pope, to be some kind of super-philosopher, having at his disposal more cogent arguments than could possibly be found elsewhere, and only entitled to speak on the basis of these.

The promises made to Peter were not of that kind.

Neo-Modernism, in the sense just indicated, is certainly a conspicuous element in the Catholic scene today and can be seen (within limits) as a kind of theology. The question therefore arises of its intellectual and academic respectability, and all the more pointedly in view of the crucial importance which it gives to intellectuals and academic people and to their characteristic and necessary kind of "freedom". Nobody desires the neo-Modernist to be actually silenced. But is there any basis upon which he can expect his transcendental utterances to be taken seriously by responsible thinkers?

The question is a real one, and two possible answers to it can be ruled out at once on lines already indicated.

In the first place, the neo-Modernist—like any other theologian—cannot make any possible transcendental utterance on the basis of his erudition alone, his learning, his scholarship: nor can he invoke any similarly-based consensus of his colleagues. This is not an arbitrary prohibition but a logical necessity, stemming directly from the limitations of human experience and human reasoning.

In the second place, the neo-Modernist—like any other theologian—needs to take something in the nature of "faith" for his starting-point and subject-matter, the firm ground upon which he bases his explorations and findings. This cannot itself be fully provable, but it does need to be clearly and frankly set forth, as the neo-Modernist's faith-position seldom is. But one thing is clear: whatever it may be, his faith-position is *not* to be equated with Catholicism as traditionally understood, and as understood in our time by such very different people as myself

and the pope, not to mention Vatican II and millions upon millions of the faithful. To Catholicism as so understood, the neo-Modernist does
not give the assent of faith. He gives his critically
selective assent to many or most elements within
it, while denying it to others on some basis which
never quite gets spelled out. He also, in his way—
although in very different language—distinguishes
the True Faith from the pernicious heresies. But
whatever his criterion of transcendental truth may
be, it is certainly not that of the Church.

This question of the neo-Modernist's intellectual and academic respectability seems to me to
be an unanswered one. In the media and over
large areas of popular consciousness, it gets by-
passed by two happy but unrealistic assumptions.
It is taken for granted that the expert always
knows best, and that a theologian is an expert on
God and things of God in exactly the same sense
as that in which a biologist is an expert on biology;
it is also taken for granted that in theology as in
the natural sciences, the newest thinking will normally be the best thinking. And if it ever seems
possible to represent the theologian as a bold
pioneer who suffers persecution at the hands of
reactionary Church authority, he will automati-
cally seem to acquire not only respectability as a
thinker but also nobility as a kind of martyr.

The question cannot really be answered as simply as all that.

About the real basis of the neo-Modernist's thinking, the criterion which he actually uses in transcendental matters, I find myself tempted—by his own habitual manner of speaking—to a rather unhappy conclusion: I would be glad to be proved wrong about this.

Despite the frequently sceptical substructure of his mind, the neo-Modernist does not hesitate to make transcendental utterances, incapable of empirical or scholarly verification, with extreme assurance: I have cited three instances of this and could cite many more. And if these utterances are challenged from the Catholic side, it is usual for him to respond in a way which I find highly revealing. Put before him some matter of faith and morals which is integral to the Catholic Faith but uncongenial to himself and his friends: characteristically, he will brush it aside with some such dismissive words as "Oh, but we just don't think like that any more!" or "That way of looking at things is completely outmoded."

Fashion is an extremely powerful determinant of human behaviour and even of belief: there are many people for whom it is far more important to be up-to-date and with the trend than to be right. It is similarly to be expected that clever people will sometimes seek to dominate on the basis of their individual or collective cleverness, even in matters about which autonomous human cleverness can tell us practically nothing. But in neither of these tendencies do we see human nature at its best. The former is an instance of what used to be called the sin of "worldliness": the latter is an instance of the sin of pride.

Few of us are in a position to cast the first stone in respect of either tendency. But we shall frequently need to take both into account, in simple realism though not in anger or contempt, when we desire to form an appraisal of some human and historical development within the Church or elsewhere.

That fluid and selective Catholicism which I and others call "neo-Modernism" has been a conspicuous thing for some fifteen years now: as a human and historical development it is possibly on the wane, and it may eventually seem capable of being described in terms of post-Conciliar trauma. But it is important for my present subject, because it provides the *only* intellectual and psychological framework within which—given the most generally Catholic premises—"Church authority" can seem antithetical to "intellectual freedom". Reject all neo-Modernism, return to the traditional faith and morals of the Church: it will then turn out that there simply isn't any problem of that kind after all.

I believe that we should reject all neo-Modernism anyway, and not on some blindly fideistic basis: it seems to me to lack intellectual respectability, by the sceptic's standards and not only by the pope's. I would be very glad to find that its faith-position, its criterion of transcendental truth, had some more solid basis than the two all-too-human failings that I have mentioned, not without uneasy memories of personal guilt. But this more solid basis, if it exists, is distinctly elusive.

It will have been noticed that I am offering little more than a specialised elaboration of the old familiar distinction between reason and revelation. Human reason can operate fruitfully upon any possible kind of subject-matter. But unless helped and guided and even informed by some transcendental agency, it can arrive at little or no transcendental certainty. It is therefore logically as well as doctrinally impossible that the Catholic Church should be or become something in which its own intelligentsia—operating as such—can play the instructive and corrective role which is played by learned experts in other fields. The theologian can ask good and penetrating questions about faith and morals: he can also devise, and submit for the Church's consideration, what may well turn out to be profound and even definitive answers to such questions. And in these activities—with due regard to the human and pastoral responsibilities which I mentioned earlier—he needs to enjoy total intellectual and academic freedom: this must not be denied him.

But he may go further: he may attempt to answer some such question definitively and on his own account and in flat contradiction of the Church's mind, as already expressed in formal terms. If he does so, he will find his path blocked by an angel with a flaming sword.

But this angel was not put there by the Inquisition: he was put there by the harsher power of Reason, with the sceptic's warm approval.

In the light of these considerations, let us consider two horrible things that might happen to some scholar or scientist, his field being left unspecified.

He has used his necessary academic freedom well, let us say: he has formed some hypothesis of great interest and (if and when verified) of great practical importance. Being human, he is deeply attached to it: he would like to see it accepted everywhere. But fate intervenes.

It can intervene in two ways, similar in one sense, but radically different in another sense which is crucial for my subject. (But he may not notice the difference: either way, he is going to be unhappy and perhaps angry.)

The first intervention of fate will come from *outside* his subject-matter. Two members of the Party Thought-Police (let us say) will visit him at home, speaking politely but in tones of unmistakable menace. This hypothesis of his, they will say, is ideologically at variance with the Party line and thus unacceptable: it would be highly prudent of him, therefore, to retract it or at least keep silent about it. The wisest policy would be for him to go back to his books and reconsider it all and come up with some more correct hypothesis. Naturally, nobody desires to threaten him! But any self-centered contumaciousness in this matter might well have very unfortunate consequences: most regrettably, our scholar might find himself deprived of his post and his degrees and his honours, silenced as regards publication and any other dissemination of his incorrect thought, and perhaps exiled like Dr. Sakharov to some remote and isolated city beyond all contact with the outside world—that is, if he's lucky. The choice is entirely his, of course: nobody wishes to interfere with his academic freedom.

Such an intrusion would indeed make the scholar unhappy and angry, and no less so by reason of that supposed "choice", even though this would be real in a way.

But let us now imagine another kind of intervention, one that comes from *inside* his subject-matter though still through human intermediaries. He publishes his hypothesis, and it arouses great interest: he feels happy, sure of himself and his acceptance and fame. But it is then pointed out to him, truthfully but infuriatingly, that he has forgotten or overlooked some crucial data—the epoch-making experiments that were recently performed by Dr. Trombonius at Uppsala, let us say, or (as the case may be) the newly-discovered and unquestionably authentic Codex of Hippo-potamopolis. This comes as an unpleasant shock to him: he naturally challenges this evidence with all he's got. But it's no good: once again, we have witnessed what Thomas Henry Huxley called "the great tragedy of science—the slaying of a beautiful hypothesis by an ugly fact."

In a sense, the effect upon the scholar or scientist in question will be much the same in either of these two cases. Either way, something outside him will be telling him to stop saying what he wants to say. The sanctions imposed upon him if he goes on saying it will be violent in the one case and only a matter of academic reputation in the other. But even there, they will still be sanctions, possibly damaging to his career; and if he is paranoid by temperament, he may be disposed to interpret this latter case in terms that would only be appropriate to the former. "I'm surrounded by enemies! They're trying to do me down!"

But the two cases are clearly different. There has been an unjust intrusion upon his academic and intellectual freedom in the one case but not in the other; and if he protests against that second intervention in quasi-legal terms—complaining, perhaps, that he has been denied "due process" and a fair hearing—he will be talking wildly. He spoke up freely and submitted himself to judgment when he advanced that hypothesis in the first place: if this breaks down when tested against the hard realities of his subject-matter, he can be understandably disappointed but he suffers no injustice.

The Michelson–Morley experiment yielded a negative result and so paved the way for relativity-theory. But if any believer in the luminiferous aether saw that experiment and its outcome as a tyrannical intrusion upon his intellectual and academic freedom, his would be a thoroughly paranoid response.

"The mind of the Church" lies within the subject-matter of the Catholic theologian and indeed constitutes the whole of it, apart from the limited field of "natural theology" and whatever else he may consider under the title of "religious studies" of the more man-centered and descriptive kind.

That Church authority has sometimes acted according to the first of the two "models" which I have just proposed, I do not in the least deny: nor do I wish to defend such actions in any positive way, though I take their undesirability to be somewhat less total than the liberal mind of today instinctively supposes.

But to the degree of its formally definitive character, a doctrinal intervention on the part of the Church—as represented, upon occasion, by the pope of the day and by those authorised to act on his behalf—will in principle be of the kind suggested by my second "model". It will be one among various possible instances of what the theologian is supposed to be studying and taking fully into account, "the mind of the Church";

and if he contradicts this in any firm and final way, he will be dogmatising beyond the limits of his own intellectual competence, and sinning therefore against the academic code no less than against the Catholic code. He will resemble some scholar who blindly, stubbornly clings to an exploded hypothesis. Such a man will be an embarrassment to his colleagues.

I thus conclude that in principle, there is no necessary conflict or tension between Church authority and the intellectual freedom of the Catholic theologian or thinker, apart from the accidental and human tension which can sometimes arise in the court-room as between the witness and the interrogating lawyer. These two are not enemies: they just have different tasks.

The limits of these need to be respected. When I next come to trial on some capital charge, I very much hope that the prosecuting lawyer does not over-ride my chief defence witness and decide the case for himself. If he attempts anything of that kind, I very much hope that he isn't allowed to get away with it. He wasn't there, after all; and the witness was.

The Judge can be trusted to see through any such attempt.